So Delish!

Simone Anderson

SUPER EASY, FRESH MEALS FOR EVERY DAY

ALLEN&UNWIN
SYDNEY · MELBOURNE · AUCKLAND · LONDON

To my beautiful friends, my family and my rock, Trent.
Thank you for backing me through every new adventure I go
on—I am forever grateful for your constant love and support.

Contents

INTRODUCTION

My weight-loss journey began on 29 August 2014. I was 23 years old and had finally found the courage to find a set of commercial scales that would read my weight—and step on them. The number staring back at me was 169 kg. That was it: that was the number that finally gave me the push I needed to change my life once and for all.

Over the next five years I flipped my entire world on its head, changing my exercise habits and training myself to think differently about food and nutrition. I started off simply, and have continued in that vein. I promised myself that I would never count another calorie and that I was going to change my lifestyle, not just go on diet number 151. I knew that in order to succeed I needed to find a way of eating that I could maintain for the rest of my life—no quick fixes and no limiting of food groups. Instead, I would aim for balance in what I ate as well as in my mindset. The cravings were crippling initially, but as each month passed I found myself wanting foods that would fuel and nourish my body, instead of seeking sugar highs.

My ethos around food and my outlook on life are clear throughout this book. I believe in balance above all else; that means finding a happy medium that works for you. There's no diet mentality here—just delicious wholesome meals for you and your family. I wanted to make sure that my recipes were cost-effective, and

that every ingredient could be found in your local supermarket. No special trips to specialty stores required, and no hunting down a random bottle of sauce that you can't pronounce the name of and will never use again! I also wanted to ensure that anyone would feel comfortable giving my recipes a go, so there are no multi-page recipes or complicated instructions. Just simple, yummy meals you actually want to cook.

For me, food has always been a big part of family life. I grew up with a mother who was a baker and an incredible cook, so my love of food developed at a very young age. Some of my earliest memories are of standing next to Mum on a little stool, helping her prepare our family dinners. I'm sure I was far more of a hindrance than a help, but Mum was always so patient with me and I learnt then many skills that I still use today. I also have my grandmother to thank for my love of food and cooking; we spent a lot of time together when I was growing up and I will always be thankful for those special memories. Gran has the best 'give anything a go' attitude, especially when it comes to cooking and baking. Her creations always taste great.

This book is filled with some of my all-time favourite recipes, many of which you will have seen on my social media pages over the years. I've also included our best-loved family recipes, as well as ones inspired by friends. The most popular content on my social media is always food-related, so creating a cookbook that brings all my recipes together in a beautiful easy-to-read format has been a long-held dream of mine. I love the idea of leaving a legacy of recipes for my (fingers crossed!) kids and grandkids.

One thing I wasn't prepared for was the emotional aspect of making a cookbook. There were so many tears; so much laughter and joy. This book means more to me than you can imagine—it shows my relationship with food coming full circle, and I am so proud to share it with the world. Many of the recipes are inspired by loved ones in my life, each of whom has helped me in some way, shape or form.

Food is here to nourish us, to energise us and to bring us closer together. When used and treated with respect, food should enrich our lives and make each day more vibrant and exciting. I hope you enjoy using this book as much as I have enjoyed making it for you.

Breakfast

SPICED PORRIDGE

SERVES **2** • TIME TO MAKE **10 MINUTES**

1 cup rolled oats
2 cups low-fat milk
1 teaspoon each ground
   cardamom and ground cinnamon
2 small bananas, peeled and sliced
8 strawberries, hulled and halved
2 tablespoons chopped pistachios
2 teaspoons runny honey
edible flowers, to garnish
   (optional)

Recently, I was away skiing for the weekend in Ohakune with friends and I suggested porridge for breakfast. There were a few eye-rolls, and one friend even protested that he would just do his own thing. As we were plating up, I heard a little voice say, 'Maybe I will try some . . . this doesn't look like the porridge Mum forced us to eat as a kid!' This certainly isn't your basic watery porridge from your childhood; my version is so tasty and warming. It's time to give porridge another go.

You can replace the strawberries with other fruit, depending on the season.

Place the oats, milk and spices in a saucepan over low heat. Cook, stirring often, for about 5 minutes, or until the porridge is creamy and bubbling.

Divide the porridge between bowls and top with banana, strawberries and pistachios. Drizzle with honey, garnish with edible flowers, if using, and serve immediately.

MIXED FRUIT PROTEIN SMOOTHIE

SERVES **2** • TIME TO MAKE **5 MINUTES**

3 cups coconut water
1 cup frozen berries
2 frozen bananas, sliced
1 cup fresh or frozen mango pieces
2 passionfruit, pulp only, or
  2 tablespoons passionfruit syrup
2 tablespoons vanilla protein
  powder

TO GARNISH (OPTIONAL)
coconut flakes
mint leaves
edible flowers

Since beginning my weight-loss journey five years ago, I start my day with a protein smoothie 90 per cent of the time. It's super quick to make, you can have it on the go, and best of all it's packed full of protein to keep you satisfied until lunch. Keep it interesting by switching up the fruits you use throughout the year depending on what's in season. I like to peel and slice bananas and keep them in the freezer for an easy base.

Place all the ingredients in a blender and blitz until smooth and creamy.

Pour into tall glasses, garnish with coconut chips, mint leaves and edible flowers, if using, and drink immediately.

PEANUT BUTTER PROTEIN SHAKE

SERVES **2** • TIME TO MAKE **5 MINUTES**

3 cups liquid of your choice
   (e.g. milk, coconut water, almond
   milk, water)
2 frozen bananas, sliced
2 tablespoons vanilla protein
   powder
2 tablespoons peanut butter
1 cup oats
pinch of ground cinnamon, to
   garnish

I confess . . . I AM A PEANUT BUTTER ADDICT AND I DO NOT WANT HELP! So to fuel my addiction and to satisfy those cravings I created this smoothie. The combination of the oats and peanut butter will make this your new fave— it's the perfect recipe to get you through the morning with a pep in your step.

Place all the ingredients except the cinnamon in a blender and blitz until smooth and creamy.

Pour into tall glasses, garnish with ground cinnamon and serve immediately.

SALMON ON TOAST

SERVES **2** • TIME TO MAKE **10 MINUTES**

2 teaspoons horseradish
⅓ cup ricotta
1 teaspoon wholegrain mustard
1 tablespoon chopped chives
4 slices Vogel's bread, toasted
1 avocado, peeled and sliced
1 radish, very thinly sliced
100 g (3½ oz) cold-smoked
   salmon slices
½ small red onion, very thinly
   sliced
1 teaspoon mixed sesame seeds,
   toasted
sea salt and freshly ground black
   pepper to taste
½ lemon, cut into wedges

We all know Vogel's bread: it's an absolute Kiwi classic, with expats filling their suitcases after every trip home to ensure they can get their breakfast fix. Here's a recipe to make it even more mouthwatering.

Mix together the horseradish, ricotta, mustard and chives, and spread over the toast. Layer over the avocado, radish, salmon and red onion.

Sprinkle over the sesame seeds, season, and serve with lemon wedges for squeezing.

VEGE OMELETTE

SERVES **1** • TIME TO MAKE **10 MINUTES**

2 teaspoons rice bran oil
2 teaspoons butter
½ red onion, diced
2 truss tomatoes, diced
1 cup spinach, roughly chopped
1 cup sliced button mushrooms
sea salt and freshly ground black
 pepper to taste
4 eggs, lightly whisked

TO SERVE

salad greens
Vogel's bread, toasted

This omelette is one of those meals I never get sick of. It's packed with everything you need to fuel you through the morning, and is quick and simple to whip up. This easy method ensures you actually end up with an omelette rather than scrambled eggs. It's great for using up leftover veges from the fridge too.

Heat half the oil and half the butter in a medium-sized non-stick frying pan until bubbling. Add the onion, tomato, spinach and mushrooms to the pan, season and cook for 5 minutes until golden and tender. Remove from the pan.

Heat the remaining oil and butter in the same pan. Pour the eggs into the pan and leave to cook for 2 minutes. Carefully spoon the vegetables over the egg, then fold the omelette in half over the veges. Reduce the heat and continue to cook for another minute until golden and set.

Cut the omelette in half and serve with salad greens and Vogel's toast.

LOADED CAULIFLOWER PANCAKES

SERVES **4** • TIME TO MAKE **25 MINUTES**

1 cauliflower, cut into florets
2 eggs, whisked
¼ cup finely grated Parmesan
¼ cup chopped chives
1 teaspoon garlic powder
sea salt and freshly ground black
   pepper to taste
2 tablespoons olive oil
1 cup grated Edam
2 cups baby spinach
8 slices champagne ham
2 large tomatoes, sliced

TO SERVE (OPTIONAL)

tomato relish
chopped parsley

These pancakes are so mouthwateringly delicious . . . the recipe says that it serves four, but if I'm perfectly honest Trent and I demolish the whole lot between two of us. But maybe you have more self-control than we do!

Place the cauliflower in a large bowl and pour over enough boiling water to cover. Leave for 3–4 minutes until just beginning to become tender. Drain well, then transfer to a food processor. Add the eggs, Parmesan, chives, garlic powder and seasoning and blitz until combined.

Heat half the oil in a large frying pan over medium heat and place 4 large spoonfuls of the batter into the pan—you want the pancakes to be about 10 cm (4 in) in diameter. Cook for 2–3 minutes until golden then flip, cover with Edam, lower the heat and wait for the cheese to melt. Remove from the pan and keep warm. Repeat with the remaining mix.

Place the cooked pancakes on plates and top with the spinach, ham and tomato. Serve immediately with a little relish and parsley, if using.

BREAKFAST BOWL

½ cup quinoa, rinsed
2 eggs
1 tablespoon olive oil
4 thick slices halloumi
sea salt and freshly ground black
   pepper to taste
4 large field mushrooms, sliced
120 g (4¼ oz) spinach
1 avocado, peeled and sliced
10 cherry tomatoes, halved
1 Lebanese cucumber, peeled
   into ribbons
2 tablespoons Hummus (see
   page 84)
1 tablespoon each toasted
   pine nuts, sliced almonds and
   pumpkin seeds
juice of 1 lime

On a recent trip to Sydney I ate at so many incredible cafés, and I kept noticing fresh, healthy breakfast bowls on every menu. I absolutely loved the concept of throwing all your favourite foods in a bowl and serving it up for breakfast, so I created my own version. Don't feel like you need to stick too closely to the recipe on this one: get creative and make it your own.

Bring a large saucepan of water to the boil. Add the quinoa and cook, stirring occasionally, for 12–15 minutes. Drain, rinse and drain well again.

Bring a small pot of water to the boil. Reduce the heat, carefully lower the eggs into the water and cook for 8 minutes, then drain and cover with cold water. Once cool enough to handle, peel and halve the eggs.

While the eggs and quinoa are cooking, heat the oil in a non-stick pan over medium heat. Cook the halloumi until golden brown on both sides. Set aside.

Season the mushrooms then, in the same pan, sauté them for 3–4 minutes.

Divide the quinoa between serving bowls. Arrange the remaining ingredients over the top, season, squeeze over the lime juice and serve.

CRUMBED ASPARAGUS WITH POACHED EGGS

1 cup plain flour
½ teaspoon sea salt
freshly ground black pepper to
   taste
4 eggs
2 teaspoons Dijon mustard
1 cup panko crumbs
2 cloves garlic, minced
½ cup finely grated Parmesan
2 bunches asparagus (about
   400 g/14 oz)

TO SERVE

2 tablespoons tomato relish or
   chutney of your choice
¼ cup chopped parsley leaves

How to spice up your simple poached egg? Pop it on a panko-crumbed asparagus base. This dish is always a crowd favourite and even gets non-asparagus eaters excited to give it a go. Asparagus is a super simple vegetable to grow in your own garden, requiring minimal love and attention— my kind of home gardening.

Preheat the oven to 200°C (400°F) and line an oven tray with baking paper.

Line up 3 large plates or shallow bowls. On the first, mix the flour, salt and pepper; on the second whisk 2 of the eggs and the mustard together; on the third, mix the crumbs, garlic and Parmesan.

Pass the asparagus spears first through the flour, then the egg, then the crumb mixture. Place on the prepared oven tray in a single layer. Bake for 10–12 minutes, or until golden and crisp.

While the asparagus is cooking, bring a large pan of water to a gentle boil and poach the remaining 2 eggs to your liking.

Serve the asparagus topped with poached egg and relish. Garnish with parsley before serving.

BREAKFAST EGG MUFFINS

MAKES **12** • TIME TO MAKE **25 MINUTES**

olive oil spray
8 eggs, whisked
1 potato (about 150 g/5½ oz),
   peeled and grated
½ red capsicum, deseeded and
   finely diced
1 cup chopped baby spinach
2 spring onions, thinly sliced
½ cup finely grated Parmesan
sea salt and freshly ground black
   pepper to taste
pinch of cayenne pepper
¼ teaspoon garlic powder
handful fresh thyme
12 cherry tomatoes, halved

This is an ideal recipe to make up on meal-prep day. Eat a few muffins fresh of course (you can't not), then pop the rest into the freezer for an easy weekday breakfast or snack. They'll defrost on their own in an hour, or you can put them in the microwave to speed up the process. Packed full of veges as well as protein from the eggs, they make a great healthy breakfast. Kids love them too.

Preheat the oven to 180°C (350°F) and lightly spray the holes of a muffin pan with cooking spray.

Place all the ingredients except the thyme and tomatoes in a bowl and mix together. Divide the mixture among the holes of the muffin pan and top each with some thyme and two tomato halves.

Bake for 12–15 minutes, or until golden and set. These keep well in the fridge and are great for when you're on the run.

CORN FRITTERS
WITH TOMATO SALSA

SERVES **4** • TIME TO MAKE **20 MINUTES**

TOMATO SALSA

2 tomatoes, diced
½ red onion, finely diced
1 green chilli, deseeded and thinly
   sliced
juice of 1 lime
¼ cup chopped coriander leaves

CORN FRITTERS

½ cup flour
1 teaspoon baking powder
2 eggs, whisked
400 g (14 oz) can creamed corn
400 g (14 oz) can whole kernel
   corn
2 tablespoons chopped parsley
   leaves, plus extra to garnish
sea salt and freshly ground black
   pepper to taste
2 tablespoons vegetable oil for
   cooking

TO SERVE

2 cups rocket leaves
1 avocado, peeled and sliced
¼ cup plain unsweetened yoghurt
1 lime, cut into wedges

Whether you're treating friends for breakfast or creating a special meal for the family, classic corn fritters are simple to whip up, yet make you look like a professional chef. The best bit is that the more rustic your fritters look the better—we're not aiming for perfection here. You'll never want to order fritters from a café again once you realise how easy they are to create at home.

Preheat the oven to 100°C (200°F) and line an oven tray with baking paper.

For the salsa, mix all the ingredients together in a bowl and set aside.

For the fritters, sift the flour and baking powder into a mixing bowl. Add the remaining ingredients, except the oil, and mix until combined.

Heat a little of the oil in a non-stick frying pan over medium-high heat. In batches, place large spoonfuls of the mixture into the pan and cook for 2 minutes, or until bubbles appear on the surface. Flip the fritters and cook for another couple of minutes until the fritters are cooked through. Place the cooked fritters on the prepared oven tray and put in the oven to keep warm. Repeat in batches, adding more oil to the pan as necessary.

Serve the fritters with tomato salsa, rocket, avocado, a dollop of yoghurt, and lime wedges for squeezing. Garnish with parsley before serving.

BREAKFAST BURRITOS

SERVES **4** • TIME TO MAKE **20 MINUTES**

BURRITOS

olive oil spray
2 low-fat pork sausages
1 red onion, diced
4 eggs, lightly beaten
400 g (14 oz) can Mexican chilli
  beans
2 small tomatoes, diced
1 cup chopped baby spinach
¼ cup chopped coriander leaves,
  plus extra to serve
½ cup grated low-fat Cheddar
sea salt and freshly ground black
  pepper to taste
4 large wholegrain wraps

GUACAMOLE

1 avocado, peeled
1 small tomato, diced
½ red onion
2 tablespoons chopped coriander
  leaves

TO SERVE

¼ cup sour cream
chipotle or Tabasco sauce
1 spring onion, sliced

Now this looks like a good time! For a different way to start your day, go with a breakfast fiesta. There's no better way to feed a crowd for breakfast than with this fun recipe, which proves that a burrito is appropriate at any time of the day.

Heat a large pan over high heat, spray with oil and squeeze small nuggets of pork mince out of the sausage skins and into the pan. Discard the skins. Cook the pork for 2 minutes, then add the red onion and continue to cook for 3–4 minutes. Add the eggs, beans, tomato, spinach, coriander and Cheddar. Cook, stirring occasionally, for another 3–4 minutes.

Season the mixture and divide among the wraps, placing it in the centre. Fold each wrap to enclose the mix. Wipe out the pan, then return the wraps to the pan and cook for 2–3 minutes on each side until golden brown.

For the guacamole, mash the avocado in a bowl, then stir through the tomato, red onion and coriander and season.

Serve the burritos topped with guacamole, sour cream, chipotle or Tabasco sauce, spring onion and extra coriander.

Lunch

ZUCCHINI NOODLES WITH PRAWNS

SERVES **4** • TIME TO MAKE **25 MINUTES**

6 small zucchini, spiralised
6 tablespoons Pistachio Pesto
  (see page 152)
2 Lebanese cucumbers, peeled
  into ribbons
100 g (3½ oz) rocket
2 tablespoons toasted pine nuts
1 punnet cherry tomatoes
3 cloves garlic, minced
1 tablespoon balsamic vinegar
sea salt and freshly ground black
  pepper to taste
2 tablespoons olive oil
1 teaspoon butter
400 g (14 oz) prawns, defrosted
  if frozen
½ cup pomegranate arils
1 lemon, cut into wedges

Zoodles: zucchini made into noodles. An absolute craze that hit the internet a couple of years back, and that's where I first discovered this pasta alternative. I still can't get Trent to eat an entire meal with zoodles as the base, but he is now at half zoodles and half pasta so that's good enough for me. Personally, I prefer them to noodles and they make my stomach much happier.

Place the zucchini in a large bowl and cover with boiling water for 30 seconds. Drain well and toss together with the pesto, cucumber, rocket and pine nuts.

Place the tomatoes, garlic, balsamic vinegar, salt, pepper and half the olive oil in a bowl and toss together.

Heat the butter and the remaining tablespoon of oil in a large frying pan over high heat. Add the prawns and cook for 2–3 minutes until pink and cooked through. Remove the prawns from the pan and add to the zucchini mixture.

Add the tomatoes to the still-hot pan and cook until just beginning to burst. Add these to the bowl with the zucchini and prawns and carefully toss together.

Transfer everything to a large serving dish or serving bowls, and scatter over the pomegranate arils. Serve hot or cold with lemon wedges for squeezing.

HALLOUMI TOAST STACK

SERVES **2** • TIME TO MAKE **10 MINUTES**

1 tablespoon vegetable or rice
  bran oil
4 thick slices halloumi
⅓ cup Hummus (see page 84)
2 slices Vogel's sandwich bread,
  toasted
100 g (3½ oz) rocket leaves
1 avocado, peeled and sliced
6 slices tinned beetroot
2 truss tomatoes, sliced
½ cup mung bean sprouts
sea salt and freshly ground black
  pepper to taste
1 tablespoon good-quality olive oil
1 tablespoon balsamic glaze
coriander leaves, to garnish

To me this is one of the best flavour combinations in the world. For the past few years I have eaten this for lunch at least once or twice a week, and I am yet to get sick of this simple but yummy dish. When I am feeling extra hungry I will bulk up the veges on the stack. If you're really ravenous, like Trent after a big day at work, you might be able to handle two stacks . . .

Heat the vegetable oil in a non-stick frying pan over medium heat. Cook the halloumi until golden brown on both sides. Set aside.

Spread the hummus on the toast, then assemble the stacks by layering rocket, avocado, beetroot, tomato and halloumi on the toast. Top with sprouts, season, drizzle over olive oil and balsamic glaze, and garnish with coriander before serving.

ROAST CHICKEN AND FETA SALAD

SERVES **4** • TIME TO MAKE **10 MINUTES**

500 g (1 lb 2 oz) sliced roast
  chicken, skin removed
½ cucumber, sliced
1 head iceberg lettuce, torn
1 red capsicum, deseeded and
  sliced
1 large carrot, peeled into ribbons
150 g (5½ oz) feta, crumbled
½ red onion, thinly sliced
2 spring onions, sliced

TO SERVE

2 tablespoons olive oil
juice of 1 lemon
4 eggs, poached
2 tablespoons balsamic glaze
sea salt and freshly ground black
  pepper to taste

This is a great way to use up leftover chicken after a roast, but it's also so much more than that. Looking at this recipe beautifully presented on the pages of *my own cookbook* (did I really just say that?), I have tears rolling down my face. A chicken and feta salad was the first meal I made for myself after I decided to change my lifestyle once and for all. It didn't look anything like this one, but that salad was me saying to all my friends and family: 'I am going to do this, I am going to get healthy and save my life.'

I can't quite believe that five years on I am down 92 kg. The word that sums up my current feeling is *proud*. I am so proud of how far I have come and what I have achieved. This recipe is my full circle, and I hope you enjoy a fancier version of the salad that was the start of my new life.

Place all the ingredients in a large bowl and toss together.

Transfer to a large serving dish or divide among bowls and drizzle with olive oil and lemon juice. Top the salad with the poached eggs, drizzle over the balsamic glaze, season and serve.

SALMON SALAD

SERVES **2** • TIME TO MAKE **10 MINUTES**

LEMON DRESSING

2 tablespoons olive oil
zest and juice of 1 lemon
sea salt and freshly ground black
  pepper to taste

SALAD

1 teaspoon sesame oil
2 x 100 g (3½ oz) salmon fillets
1 lemon, halved
½ cup frozen shelled edamame
  beans, defrosted and rinsed
1 head lettuce, leaves torn
2 tomatoes, sliced
½ avocado, peeled and sliced
100 g (3½ oz) feta, crumbled
2 tablespoons toasted seeds (e.g.
  sesame, pumpkin and sunflower)
¼ cup parsley leaves
1 spring onion, sliced

When you are pushed for time but still want a super tasty lunch, this is the one to go for. With all your essential fatty acids and a decent serving of avocado, it's good for you as well as tasting great. The toasted seeds add a nice texture. For an even faster version use hot-smoked salmon fillets and fresh lemon.

For the dressing, place all the ingredients in a small jar and shake together until combined. Set aside.

For the salad, heat the sesame oil in a griddle pan or frying pan over medium-high heat. Cook the salmon for 2 minutes on each side. Remove from the pan and set aside.

Place the lemon halves in the hot pan, cut side down, and cook until starting to caramelise.

Steam or microwave the edamame beans for 2 minutes. Place the lettuce, tomato, avocado, edamame and feta in a bowl and toss together.

Transfer the salad to serving bowls. Remove the skin from the salmon and discard. Break up the salmon fillets over the top of the salad and drizzle over the dressing.

Garnish the salad with the seeds, parsley and spring onion, before serving with the grilled lemon on the side.

CHICKEN POKÉ BOWL

SERVES **2** • TIME TO MAKE **25 MINUTES**

TERIYAKI SAUCE

¼ cup soy sauce
¼ cup mirin
1 cup water
2 tablespoons brown sugar
2 cloves garlic, minced
4 cm (1½ in) piece fresh ginger,
   finely grated

POKÉ BOWL

½ cup brown rice
2 chicken thighs, sliced
½ cup frozen shelled edamame
   beans, defrosted and rinsed
½ red capsicum, deseeded and
   sliced
½ carrot, peeled and grated
2 radishes, very thinly sliced
¼ red cabbage, thinly shredded
1 Lebanese cucumber, peeled into
   ribbons
½ avocado, peeled and sliced
sea salt and freshly ground black
   pepper to taste

GARNISHES

¼ cup coriander leaves
1 spring onion, thinly sliced
2 tablespoons coconut chips
2 teaspoons toasted sesame seeds

You would have noticed poké joints popping up all around you over the past few years. I can see why this craze took off: a good poké bowl tastes delish and is full of goodness to sustain you over the day. But you don't need to fork out crazy money to enjoy one—they are super simple to make at home and can be prepared ahead to save on time.

The teriyaki sauce recipe makes plenty, and you can keep any extra in the fridge for up to 2 weeks.

For the teriyaki sauce, place all the ingredients in a small saucepan and cook over medium heat for 10 minutes. Set aside.

Cook the brown rice according to the packet instructions and set aside to cool.

Place the chicken and ¼ cup of the teriyaki sauce in a bowl and stir to coat. Heat a non-stick frying pan over high heat, add the chicken and cook for 2–3 minutes each side until the chicken is cooked through, sticky and tender.

Steam or microwave the edamame beans for 2 minutes. Divide all the poké bowl ingredients between serving bowls and top with the garnishes. I sometimes like to serve with lime wedges and sriracha sauce on the side.

GREEK-STYLE ZUCCHINI FRITTATA

SERVES **4–6** • TIME TO MAKE **45 MINUTES**

2 large zucchini, grated
1 potato, peeled and grated
1 onion, finely chopped
2 cups baby spinach, roughly
  chopped
340 g (11 ¾ oz) jar marinated
  artichoke hearts, roughly
  chopped
8 eggs, lightly beaten
100 g (3½ oz) crumbly feta
½ cup rice flour
½ teaspoon baking powder
½ teaspoon paprika
½ cup chopped dill
½ cup chopped parsley leaves
1 teaspoon dried oregano
¼ cup olive oil
sea salt and freshly ground black
  pepper to taste
1 red capsicum, deseeded and
  thinly sliced

TO SERVE

4 cups mesclun or leafy greens
relish of your choice

Moist is not a word I like to use, and I try avoid it whenever I can. But in this case 'moist' is the best way to describe this frittata: there are no dry, bland eggs here. This dish goes down a treat with the whole family.

Preheat the oven to 180°C (350°F) and line a 20 cm x 30 cm (8 in x 12 in) brownie tin with baking paper.

Place all the ingredients, except the capsicum, in a large bowl and mix well until the flour and baking powder are fully incorporated.

Pour into the prepared tin, arrange the capsicum on top and cook for 30–35 minutes, or until the frittata is golden brown on top and set. Remove from the oven and allow to cool for 5 minutes.

Cut into portions and serve with salad leaves and a dollop of your choice of relish.

GRILLED CHICKEN AND VEGETABLE STACKS

SERVES **4** • TIME TO MAKE **30 MINUTES, PLUS 1 HOUR MARINATING TIME**

4 skinless chicken breasts, sliced
  in half lengthways
zest and juice of 1 lemon
3 cloves garlic, minced
1 tablespoon thyme leaves
4 tablespoons olive oil
sea salt and freshly ground black
  pepper to taste
2 large orange kumara, sliced into
  1 cm (½ in) rounds
2 large red capsicum, deseeded
  and quartered
2 large zucchini, sliced 1 cm (½ in)
  thick lengthways
2 eggplants, sliced 1 cm (½ in)
  thick lengthways
150 g (5½ oz) baby spinach leaves

TO SERVE
100 g (3½ oz) creamy feta
Yoghurt Sauce (see page 76)
mint leaves, to garnish

Stack, stack, baby! A twist on your basic meat-and-three-veges meal, and isn't this version so much more appealing to look at? Get in my belly now . . .

Preheat the oven to 200°C (400°F) and line 2 oven trays with baking paper.

Place the chicken in a large shallow dish and mix with the lemon zest and juice, garlic, thyme and half the olive oil. Season, then cover and refrigerate for at least 1 hour to marinate.

Lay the kumara, capsicum, zucchini and eggplant on the prepared oven trays, drizzle with the remaining 2 tablespoons of olive oil and season. Bake for 20 minutes, or until the vegetables are tender.

Heat a heavy-based frying pan or griddle pan over medium-high heat. Cook the chicken for 3–4 minutes on each side until golden brown and cooked through, then set aside to rest.

Assemble the stacks by layering the roasted vegetables, spinach and chicken on serving plates, using a skewer to keep them secure if desired. Crumble over the feta, drizzle with the yoghurt sauce and garnish with mint leaves before serving.

CAESAR SALAD

SERVES **2** • TIME TO MAKE **15 MINUTES**

CAESAR DRESSING

1 cup mayonnaise
1 teaspoon Dijon mustard
juice of 1 lemon
2 anchovies, minced
2 cloves garlic, minced
¼ cup finely grated Parmesan
sea salt and freshly ground black
   pepper to taste

SALAD

olive oil spray
4 slices rindless eye bacon
2 chicken thighs, sliced
2 baby cos lettuce, leaves roughly
   chopped
10 cherry tomatoes, halved
1 avocado, peeled and sliced
2 hard-boiled eggs, halved
¼ cup shaved Parmesan
sea salt and freshly ground black
   pepper to taste

Now I am not an anchovy fan and I struggled to add those little devils to this dish, but I do realise they're a classic component of a Caesar salad and I didn't want any hate letters so this is for the lovers! The recipe makes a lot of dressing; you can refrigerate the remainder for up to a week and use it on other salads.

For the dressing, mix all the ingredients together in a small bowl. Set aside.

For the salad, heat a large frying pan over medium-high heat. Spray with oil, add the bacon and chicken, and cook until the bacon is just crispy and the chicken is golden brown and cooked through.

Arrange the lettuce, cherry tomatoes and avocado in serving bowls, add the chicken, bacon and egg, and drizzle over the dressing. Top with the Parmesan, season and serve.

CAULIFLOWER TABBOULEH

SERVES **4** • TIME TO MAKE **10 MINUTES**

1 head cauliflower, roughly cut into
   florets
2 spring onions, sliced
1 punnet cherry tomatoes, halved
½ cucumber, finely diced
1 cup chopped parsley leaves
1 cup chopped mint leaves, plus
   extra to serve
¼ cup extra virgin olive oil
2 tablespoons lemon juice
sea salt and freshly ground black
   pepper to taste

TO SERVE

4 hard-boiled eggs, halved
100 g (3½ oz) crumbly feta
4 teaspoons sliced almonds

Vegetables make up the majority of my diet, but I haven't always eaten like this—well, that's stating the obvious, considering I once weighed 169 kg! Dishes like this tabbouleh helped me develop a new love-love relationship with everything vegetable. Now I reckon vegetables are the most vibrant and flavourful part of any dish.

Place the cauliflower in a food processor and whizz until it resembles small grains of rice.

Place the cauliflower in a large bowl with all the other ingredients and stir to combine.

Transfer to serving bowls, top with the egg, and serve scattered with crumbled feta, almonds and extra mint leaves.

CAPRESE SALAD

SERVES **4** • TIME TO MAKE **5 MINUTES**

6 large heirloom or beefsteak
   tomatoes, thickly sliced
2 large mozzarella balls, thickly
   sliced
1 cup basil leaves
1 tablespoon extra virgin olive oil
1 tablespoon balsamic glaze
flaky sea salt and freshly ground
   black pepper to taste

This salad is my Auntie Sonia in one picture. For as long as I can remember, every single family function she has hosted (which is all of them!) has featured one of her Caprese salads. Big chunky slices of tomato and mozzarella make for a beautiful-looking dish. The only concern in our family is whether you can get in there before my little cousin Frankie comes along and eats all the cheese and leaves the rest—you can't afford to muck around.

Arrange the tomato and mozzarella slices in layers on a serving dish or serving plates.

Scatter over the basil and drizzle with oil and balsamic glaze. Season and serve immediately.

BABY PIZZAS
WITH GREEK SALAD

SERVES **4–6** • TIME TO MAKE **20 MINUTES**

BABY PIZZAS

4 small wholemeal pita breads, cut
    in half horizontally
1 cup pizza sauce
100 g (3½ oz) baby spinach
1 red capsicum, deseeded and
    sliced
1 cup sliced button mushrooms
1 cup pitted kalamata olives
2 cups grated mozzarella

GREEK SALAD

½ cucumber, halved and sliced
4 small tomatoes, quartered
1 small red onion, very thinly sliced
½ cup cubed feta
½ cup parsley leaves, plus extra to
    garnish
2 tablespoons olive oil
1 tablespoon balsamic vinegar
sea salt and freshly ground black
    pepper to taste

I love reworking classic takeaway meals at home, and this recipe gives you the perfect way to satisfy your pizza cravings using fresh, healthy ingredients. I spent 14 years as a nanny, and I learned very quickly that getting the kids involved in making their favourite meals at home meant they rarely hassled me to buy them takeaways for dinner. So on Friday evenings I would get them all in the kitchen creating their own pizzas. Pita breads are a good choice for the base as the smaller size is ideal for little hands.

Preheat the oven to 200°C (400°F) and line 2 large oven trays with baking paper.

Place 4 pita bases on each prepared tray. Spread the pizza sauce over the pita bases. Divide the spinach, capsicum, mushroom and olives among the pizza bases and scatter over the mozzarella. Cook for 10–12 minutes until the cheese is golden and bubbling.

While the pizzas are cooking, place all the salad ingredients in a large bowl and toss to combine.

Garnish the pizzas with extra parsley and serve with Greek salad on the side.

CEVICHE WITH AVOCADO AND TOMATO SALSA

SERVES **4** • TIME TO MAKE **5 MINUTES, PLUS 2 HOURS MARINATING TIME**

600g very fresh firm white fish

zest and juice of 4 limes, plus extra lime wedges to serve

1 small red onion, finely chopped

1 red chilli, deseeded and thinly sliced

¼ cup coconut cream

½ cucumber, diced

2 tomatoes, diced

sea salt and freshly ground black pepper to taste

1 head cos lettuce, leaves separated to make lettuce cups

Baked Tortilla Chips, to serve (see page 150)

SALSA

1 avocado, peeled and diced

1 tomato, diced

1 cup chopped coriander leaves, plus extra to garnish ceviche (optional)

sea salt and freshly ground black pepper to taste

These little lettuce boats make for a fun way to serve fresh ceviche and salsa. When I started dating Trent four years ago I quickly discovered that seafood—and in particular ceviche—was a favourite of his. Of course I had to pretend I knew exactly how to make ceviche, and that it had always been a favourite of mine too (while running to the computer to google some recipes). I was stoked to realise that it's actually super easy to make.

Cut the fish fillets into bite-sized pieces and place in a large non-reactive bowl (stainless steel, glass, ceramic or enamel-coated bowls are fine; avoid aluminium, cast iron or copper). Add the lime zest and juice, red onion and half the chilli. Stir and place in the fridge for a couple of hours to marinate.

Remove from the fridge and stir through the coconut cream, cucumber and tomato, and season to taste. Spoon the ceviche into the lettuce cups. Garnish with coriander, if desired.

For the salsa, place the ingredients in a small bowl and stir to combine.

Serve the ceviche cups with the salsa and tortilla chips.

HALLOUMI AND COUSCOUS SALAD BOWL

SERVES **4** • TIME TO MAKE **15 MINUTES**

CUMIN DRESSING

2 tablespoons olive oil
¼ cup lemon juice
1 teaspoon ground cumin
sea salt and freshly ground black
   pepper to taste
¼ cup finely chopped parsley
   leaves, plus extra to serve

SALAD

1½ cups Israeli couscous
olive oil spray
200 g (7 oz) halloumi, sliced
1 cup frozen shelled edamame
   beans, defrosted and rinsed
100 g (3½ oz) baby rocket
2 cups cherry tomatoes, halved
1 cup strawberries, hulled and
   quartered
½ cup toasted pistachios

Halloumi . . . your girl is a tad obsessed with it. This squeaky cheese takes any dish to another level in my opinion, and on top of that it's a good source of protein. Make this salad for your next family gathering and be prepared for compliments—it's a crowd-pleaser.

For the dressing, place all the ingredients in a small jar and shake together until combined.

For the salad, bring a large pot of salted water to the boil. Add the couscous and cook until al dente, 8–10 minutes. Drain and rinse under cold water. Drain again well.

While the couscous is cooking, heat a non-stick frying pan or griddle pan over medium heat. Spray with oil and add the halloumi slices. Cook until golden on both sides and remove from the pan.

Steam or microwave the edamame beans for 2 minutes. Place the couscous, halloumi, edamame and all the remaining salad ingredients in a large bowl. Pour over the dressing and toss to combine.

Transfer to a large serving dish, scatter over some extra parsley and serve.

SALMON AND RICE

SERVES **2** • TIME TO MAKE **20 MINUTES**

½ cup brown rice
2 eggs
1 tablespoon sesame oil
2 x 150 g (5½ oz) skin-on salmon
    fillets
sea salt and freshly ground black
    pepper to taste
2 large bok choy, quartered
    lengthways
1 tablespoon sesame seeds

TO SERVE

1 avocado, peeled and sliced
coriander leaves
lemon wedges

This recipe was inspired by a dish one of my best friends, Becca, made me for dinner a few years ago. It's a staple of hers and I instantly understood why: it's full of good fats and tastes unreal. If you are super pushed for time, grab a heat-and-go packet of rice and you have lunch in 10 minutes.

Cook the brown rice according to the packet instructions.

While the rice is cooking, bring a small pot of water to the boil. Reduce the heat, carefully lower the eggs into the water and cook for 8 minutes, then drain and cover with cold water. Once cool enough to handle, peel and halve the eggs.

Heat the oil in a non-stick pan over medium heat. Season the salmon and add to the pan, skin side down. Cook for 3 minutes, or until the skin is crispy. Carefully turn the salmon over and cook for another 2 minutes. Remove from the pan and set aside to rest.

Add the bok choy to the still-hot pan, adding a little more oil if necessary. Sprinkle over the sesame seeds and cook for 2 minutes.

Arrange the rice, hard-boiled eggs and avocado on serving plates. Lay the salmon and bok choy on the rice, pour over any juices from the pan, season and garnish with coriander. Serve with lemon wedges for squeezing.

CAULIFLOWER, BROCCOLI AND PRAWN BOWL

SERVES **4** • TIME TO MAKE **25 MINUTES**

TAHINI DRESSING

2 tablespoons tahini
2 tablespoons water
¼ cup Hummus (see page 84)
¼ cup plain unsweetened yoghurt
juice of 1 lemon

SALAD

1 head cauliflower, cut into florets
1 head broccoli, cut into florets
2 medium beetroot, peeled and
   quartered
1 tablespoon olive oil, plus extra to
   drizzle
sea salt and freshly ground black
   pepper to taste
1 cup quinoa
12 prawns, defrosted if frozen
zest and juice of 1 lemon
1 teaspoon chilli flakes
100 g (3½ oz) baby spinach
½ cup walnut pieces, toasted
lemon wedges

This is one of my go-tos when I'm prepping meals ahead of time. I love whipping this up on a Sunday, knowing my lunches for the start of the week are all ready to go and there's no excuse not to eat well. Keep the dressing separate and drizzle it over just before eating to ensure the ingredients stay fresher for longer.

For the dressing, place the ingredients in a small blender and blitz. Add a little extra water if necessary to achieve the desired consistency. Set aside.

For the salad, preheat the oven to 200°C (400°F). Place the cauliflower, broccoli and beetroot in a large roasting tray, drizzle with some olive oil and season. Roast for 15–20 minutes.

While the vegetables are roasting, cook the quinoa according to the packet instructions.

Heat the 1 tablespoon olive oil in a large frying pan over high heat. Add the prawns and cook for 1 minute. Add the lemon zest and juice and chilli flakes, stir and cook for another minute until the prawns are pink. Remove from the heat.

If serving immediately, assemble all the salad ingredients on a large serving platter, drizzle over the dressing and serve with lemon wedges for squeezing. Alternatively, divide into portions and keep the dressing separate until just before eating.

CHICKEN TRAY BAKE WITH COUSCOUS

SERVES **2** • TIME TO MAKE **30 MINUTES**

3 baby beetroot, halved
1 large red onion, cut into wedges
1 large orange kumara, peeled and
 sliced into 1 cm (½ in) rounds
1 red capsicum, deseeded and cut
 into thick slices
1 large carrot, peeled and roughly
 chopped
10 cherry tomatoes
sea salt and freshly ground black
 pepper to taste
5 sprigs fresh thyme
1 lemon, sliced, plus extra lemon
 wedges to serve
4 boneless, skinless chicken thighs
 (about 300–400 g / 10½–14 oz)
2 tablespoons olive oil
½ cup couscous
pinch of paprika
2 cups rocket
250 g (9 oz) bunch broccolini
¼ cup roasted cashews

If you haven't tried couscous you must have been living under a rock, but you have also been missing out on the easiest base for your veges and meat. Couscous is super simple to prepare and bulks up any dish—it's that good they named it twice! For this recipe you can switch up the vegetables depending on what you need to use up in your fridge. You'll have a yummy lunch in no time.

Preheat the oven to 190°C (375°F) and line a large oven tray with baking paper. Bring a large pot of salted water to the boil and cover.

Place the beetroot, onion, kumara, capsicum, carrot and tomatoes on the oven tray. Season well and scatter over the thyme.

Roll the lemon slices up inside the chicken thighs and tie with some kitchen string. Place on the oven tray with the vegetables, season and drizzle everything with olive oil. Roast for 25 minutes until the chicken and vegetables are cooked through. Set the chicken aside to rest.

While the chicken and vegetables are roasting, cook the couscous according to the packet instructions. Sprinkle with the paprika and stir through. Add the couscous and rocket to the cooked vegetables and mix through.

Just before serving, plunge the broccolini into the pot of boiling water for 30 seconds then remove.

Divide the vegetables between serving plates and top with the chicken and broccolini. Scatter over the cashews and serve with lemon wedges for squeezing.

MOROCCAN LAMB OPEN BURGERS WITH HALLOUMI AND PISTACHIO PESTO

SERVES **4** • TIME TO MAKE **30 MINUTES**

YOGHURT SAUCE

1 cup Greek yoghurt
juice of 1 lemon
1 clove garlic, minced
2 tablespoons chopped mint
  leaves, plus extra to serve
½ cup finely diced cucumber
sea salt and freshly ground black
  pepper to taste

LAMB BURGERS

¼ cup milk
½ cup breadcrumbs
500 g (1 lb 2 oz) lamb mince
2 teaspoons Moroccan seasoning
¼ cup coriander leaves
½ teaspoon sea salt
½ teaspoon freshly ground black
  pepper
olive oil spray

TO SERVE

200 g (7 oz) halloumi, sliced
2 wholemeal pita breads
¼ cup tomato relish
½ iceberg lettuce, leaves washed
1 large tomato, sliced
½ cucumber, peeled into ribbons
Pistachio Pesto (see page 152)
chopped pistachios

Making a burger from scratch at home is so rewarding. I used to eat a burger at least once a day when I was at my heaviest, and it's home-cooked alternatives like this that helped change my relationship with fast food, making me realise how much better a burger made in your own kitchen with fresh ingredients can taste. I can't remember the last time I ate from a takeaway joint, and that is a pretty wicked feeling.

For the yoghurt sauce, place all the ingredients in a bowl and stir to combine. Set aside.

Preheat a barbecue grill plate or a large griddle pan over medium-high heat.

For the burgers, combine the milk and breadcrumbs in a bowl and set aside to soak for 5 minutes. Mix the lamb mince with the Moroccan seasoning, coriander, salt and pepper. Add the soaked breadcrumbs and mix well. Form four patties and spray with a little oil.

Cook the patties on the grill or in the pan for 3–4 minutes each side, or until cooked to your liking. Cover with tin foil and set aside to rest for 5 minutes. Spray the halloumi slices with oil, season and place on the grill or in the pan. Cook for 2 minutes each side, or until golden brown. Set aside.

Cut the pita breads in half horizontally and lightly toast on the grill or in the pan. Layer the relish, lettuce, tomato, lamb patties, halloumi and cucumber on top of the pita breads, then spoon over some pesto and yoghurt sauce. Scatter over a few extra pistachios and mint to serve.

Platters

'Platter Queen' is what those in my life like to call me. It's pretty self-explanatory: I just love a good platter. From prepping the food to styling it and serving it, and finally seeing every inch get demolished.

The platter 'recipes' in this chapter are just a guide to the kind of things I like to include for different occasions. There aren't any hard and fast rules, so pick and choose the bits you like best and add your own favourites.

ENTERTAINING PLATTER

SERVES **10–12**

This is such a great and cost-effective way to feed a large group when you're entertaining. You can also prepare your platters before the event, then sit back and relax alongside your guests.

- 1 cup Yoghurt Sauce (see page 76)
- 1 bunch asparagus (woody ends removed), blanched
- 10 grissini, wrapped in prosciutto
- 1 cup storebought peppadews stuffed with feta
- 10 storebought cheese straws
- 1 cup mixed olives
- 10 dried peaches
- 1 wheel Camembert
- 200 g (7 oz) cumin gouda
- 200 g (7 oz) Port Salut
- 50 g (1¾ oz) salami

- 6 vine tomatoes
- 1 bunch radishes, cut into wedges
- fresh walnuts
- cornichons
- baby cos leaves
- selection of crackers
- 1 cup blueberries
- 1 bunch each of red and green grapes
- 1 cup Hummus (see overleaf)
- Pink Pickled Onions (see overleaf)
- Mediterranean Skewers (see overleaf)
- fresh herbs to garnish (e.g. rosemary, thyme, parsley, basil, etc.)

HUMMUS

400 g (14 oz) can chickpeas
2 tablespoons lemon juice
2 tablespoons tahini
1 clove garlic
¼ cup olive oil, plus extra to garnish
¼ teaspoon sea salt
¼ teaspoon freshly ground black pepper
dukkah to garnish

Drain and rinse the chickpeas. Place in a food
processor with the lemon juice, tahini, garlic, olive
oil, sea salt and freshly ground black pepper. Blitz
until smooth. Top with a little extra olive oil and
a sprinkle of dukkah. Makes about 1 cup, and will
keep in the fridge for up to 1 week.

PINK PICKLED ONIONS

1 cup white vinegar
½ cup water
⅓ cup sugar
few cumin seeds
2 red onions, thinly sliced

Combine the white vinegar, water, sugar and
cumin seeds in a saucepan and heat until the
sugar dissolves. Add the red onion and remove
from the heat. Leave to stand overnight, then
transfer to a jar and refrigerate until needed—
they'll keep for 3–4 weeks. Serve on thinly sliced
rye bread with cheese, cornichons and fresh
thyme.

MEDITERRANEAN SKEWERS

Using a melon baller, scoop balls of rockmelon
and place them on skewers with basil leaves,
bocconcini and cherry tomatoes.

KID-FRIENDLY SNACK PLATTER

SERVES **2**

There is something about having the opportunity to pick and choose from a platter that children just love. I often find they end up eating more this way, as well as sampling a greater variety of things. Keep the items bite-sized for little hands and mouths.

- Peanut Butter and Cacao Nib Protein Bliss Balls (see page 160)
- 1 cup Hummus (see page 84)
- 1 cup pretzels
- 10 baby carrots, peeled or scrubbed
- 6 strawberries

- 1 cup blueberries
- selection of crackers or crostini
- Orange 'Hedgehog' (see overleaf)
- Egg on Your Face! (see overleaf)
- Popcorn (see overleaf)
- Fruit and Cucumber Shapes (see overleaf)

ORANGE 'HEDGEHOG'

100 g (3½ oz) Edam
4 cherry tomatoes
4 large grapes
4 pieces pineapple
8 skewers
½ orange

Cut the Edam into 24 cubes. Cut the cherry tomatoes and grapes in half (or use 8 small grapes). Use a star cookie cutter to get 4 small star shapes out of the pineapple pieces. Thread 3 pieces of cheese and 1 each of the tomato, grape and pineapple pieces onto each skewer. Poke the skewer ends into the orange half to make a hedgehog shape.

EGG ON YOUR FACE!

2 hard-boiled eggs
8 small pieces of red capsicum
4 thin slices of celery

Halve the hard-boiled eggs. Decorate the egg halves with capsicum pieces for 'eyes' and celery slices for 'smiles'. Cut any leftover capsicum and celery into batons and add to the platter, if desired.

POPCORN

¼ cup popcorn kernels
medium paper bag

Place the popcorn kernels in the paper bag and fold over the top. Microwave on high until popping slows down; this usually takes 1½–2 minutes. If there are no pops for 2 seconds or more, you're done. Carefully open the bag, watching for steam.

This is a great way of making healthy popcorn quickly. You can jazz up your popcorn by sprinkling it with spices after popping—try cinnamon for the kids or paprika for the grown-ups.

FRUIT AND CUCUMBER SHAPES

Take some small cookie cutters and cut shapes into slices of fruit—rockmelon, mango, watermelon and pineapple are popular choices. You can also slice some cucumber lengthways and cut shapes from the cucumber strips.

COUPLES' (CAN'T BE BOTHERED COOKING) PLATTER

SERVES **2**

Your next date night is sorted! This platter is the perfect thing to graze from while you're snuggling up on the couch or watching the sunset at your favourite beach. Platters are also a great way to use up leftovers from other recipes. Have fun throwing your favourite things onto a board and try not to fight over the last piece of cheese . . .

- 1 cup Ceviche (see page 64)
- 1 small packet vegetable crisps
- 4 baby cucumbers, quartered lengthways
- 1 wheel Camembert
- selection of crackers and bagel crisps
- 1 chorizo sausage, sliced
- 4–6 slices grilled halloumi

- 6 meatballs, made from the Bunless Burger recipe (see page 130)
- Sherry and Orange-glazed Salmon (see page 112) with caperberries and lemon
- 25 g (1 oz) salami
- Pistachio Pesto (see page 152)
- avocado slices
- storebought horseradish cream

MEZZE PLATTER

SERVES 6–8

Mediterranean-style food was made for platters. By assembling a few dips, some fresh veges and a couple of throw-together recipes you can showcase a whole other world of flavour.

- Hummus (see page 84) topped with olive oil and pomegranate arils
- storebought stuffed vine leaves
- 1 cup storebought taramasalata
- ¼ cup roasted pistachios
- 1 cup Yoghurt Sauce (see page 76)
- Grilled Pita Bread (see below)
- Falafel Balls (see below)

- Lemony Olives (see below)
- Charred Lemon (see below)
- Lamb Koftas (see overleaf)
- Crumbed Artichoke Hearts with Parmesan and Garlic (see overleaf)
- Charred Eggplant Rolls (see overleaf)
- Deconstructed Greek Salad (see overleaf)

GRILLED PITA BREAD

Cut pita breads into triangles, spray with olive oil and grill for 1–2 minutes.

FALAFEL BALLS

Heat a little vegetable oil in a pan and scoop tablespoonfuls of storebought falafel mix into the hot oil. Turn when golden brown.

LEMONY OLIVES

Stir 1 tablespoon finely chopped preserved lemon through 1 cup mixed olives.

CHARRED LEMON

Cut 1 lemon in half and place in a hot pan, flesh side down, until caramelised.

LAMB KOFTAS

400 g (14 oz) lamb mince
1 teaspoon ground cumin
1 clove of garlic, minced
1 tablespoon finely chopped mint leaves

Mix the ingredients together in a bowl. Scoop up a handful of mixture and shape into a cigar shape around a thick skewer or wooden chopstick. Repeat until you have used up all the mixture. Grill, turning as needed, until just cooked through, about 5 minutes. Makes about 12 koftas.

CHARRED EGGPLANT ROLLS

Thinly slice an eggplant lengthways and grill on the barbecue or in a grill pan. Roll up the slices of eggplant with marinated feta, roasted capsicum and thyme inside, and secure with skewers.

CRUMBED ARTICHOKE HEARTS WITH PARMESAN AND GARLIC

340 g (11¾ oz) jar of marinated artichoke hearts
½ cup panko crumbs
2 cloves of garlic, minced
zest of 1 lemon
¼ cup finely grated Parmesan

Preheat the oven to 180°C (350°F). Drain the artichoke hearts and set aside. In a bowl, mix together the panko crumbs, garlic, lemon zest and Parmesan. Roll the artichoke hearts in the crumb mixture. Bake for 10–15 minutes until golden and crispy.

DECONSTRUCTED GREEK SALAD

Peel 1 Lebanese cucumber into ribbons and place on the platter. Top with cubes of feta, halved cherry tomatoes and pomegranate arils.

FRUIT PLATTER

SERVES **6–8**

This fruit platter is colourful, fun and suitable for any occasion.
I have used all of my favourite fruits here, but feel free to get creative
and swap in the ones that tickle your fancy. It always pays to shop
seasonally to keep the cost down and the flavours at their best.

- 1 mango
- 1 dragonfruit, sliced
- 1 bunch each of red and green grapes
- 1 punnet strawberries, hulled and halved
- 1 punnet blueberries
- 3 tamarillos, halved
- 2 mandarins, peeled and segmented
- 1 nashi pear, cut into wedges

- 1 apple, sliced
- 1 rockmelon, peeled and cut into bite-sized chunks
- 2 green and 2 gold kiwifruit, peeled and cut into wedges
- ½ cup pomegranate arils
- 2 tablespoons runny honey
- 1 lime, cut into wedges

'Hedgehog' the mango by slicing 'cheeks' from either side of the mango stone, then carefully cutting a criss-cross pattern in the flesh, making sure not to pierce the skin at all. Carefully turn the mango cheek inside out with your thumbs to expose the little squares on the other side.

Arrange the mango with all the remaining fruit on serving plates or a large platter. Drizzle with honey and serve with lime wedges for squeezing.

Dinner

BEEF AND LENTIL CURRY

SERVES **4** • TIME TO MAKE **1 HOUR**

500 g (1 lb 2 oz) chuck steak, diced
⅓ cup storebought korma curry paste
2 tablespoons olive oil
2 cloves garlic, minced
1 onion, diced
3 cm (1¼ in) piece fresh ginger, finely grated
2 cups salt-reduced beef stock
400 ml (14 fl oz) can light coconut milk
½ cup red lentils
½ large head cauliflower, cut into florets
1 cup frozen peas
4 cups baby spinach

TO SERVE

1 cup Greek yoghurt
¼ cup finely diced cucumber
4 roti
2 cups cooked brown rice
½ cup coriander leaves
1 lemon, cut into wedges

Lentils are something I didn't try until later in life, and OMG had I been missing out. They are great for bulking up so many dishes, especially curries. This curry is full of flavour and always leaves me satisfied. It's a good dish to prep at the start of the week and keep in the freezer for work lunches—making the entire office jealous when your steaming-hot curry emerges from the microwave.

Place the beef and half the korma paste in a bowl and toss to coat. Heat half the oil in a large frying pan over medium-high heat. Add the beef to the pan and brown on all sides. Remove from the pan and set aside.

Add the remaining tablespoon of oil to the pan with the garlic, onion and ginger and cook for 2–3 minutes until fragrant. Stir in the remaining korma paste, stock, coconut milk and lentils. Bring to the boil, reduce the heat, cover and simmer for 10 minutes.

Return the beef to the pan along with the cauliflower, and continue to simmer for another 15–20 minutes until the beef is tender. Stir through the peas and spinach.

While the curry is cooking, mix the yoghurt and cucumber together in a bowl and set aside.

Divide the curry among bowls and serve with the yoghurt, cucumber, roti, rice, coriander, and lemon wedges for squeezing.

SPICY CHICKEN FRIED RICE

SERVES **4** • TIME TO MAKE **20 MINUTES**

1 tablespoon vegetable oil
500 g (1 lb 2 oz) chicken mince
2 x 250 g (9 oz) packets
  microwave rice (or 2 cups
  leftover cooked rice)
¼ cup soy sauce, plus extra to
  serve
3 cloves garlic, minced
1 carrot, peeled into ribbons
1 red capsicum, deseeded and
  chopped
234 g (8½ oz) can pineapple
  pieces
¼ teaspoon chilli flakes
1 cup frozen peas
2 eggs, lightly beaten

TO SERVE

2 spring onions, chopped
¼ cup coriander leaves
2 tablespoons toasted sesame
  seeds
1 lime, cut into wedges
2 tablespoons sriracha sauce

Quick, delicious and super simple to throw together: this dish is perfect for those evenings when you are pushed for time but still want a home-cooked meal. If you're feeding little munchkins, my best tip is to cut the veges into tiny pieces to help disguise them (and of course ditch the sriracha).

Heat the oil in a large frying pan or wok over high heat. Add the chicken mince and cook, stirring often, for 5 minutes.

Add the rice, soy sauce, garlic, carrot, capsicum, pineapple, chilli flakes and peas and cook for another 6–8 minutes, tossing or stirring occasionally.

Heat a non-stick pan over high heat. Pour the eggs into the pan and allow to set, then roll the egg pancake into a long cigar shape. Slice the rolled-up egg into long ribbons.

Divide the fried rice among serving bowls and top with egg ribbons, spring onion, coriander and sesame seeds. Serve with lime wedges for squeezing, sriracha and extra soy sauce.

LAMB KEBABS WITH HERB SALAD AND ASPARAGUS

SERVES **4** • TIME TO MAKE **45 MINUTES**

SALAD

120 g (4¼ oz) mesclun
4 radishes, thinly sliced
½ cup Italian parsley leaves
½ cup mint leaves
½ cup pomegranate arils
½ cucumber, thinly sliced
1 cup microgreens
2 tablespoons olive oil
zest and juice of 1 lemon
sea salt and freshly ground black
   pepper to taste

LAMB KEBABS

500 g (1 lb 2 oz) lamb rump, diced
1 red onion, cut into wedges
2 zucchini, thickly sliced
1 red capsicum, deseeded and
   chopped into chunks
2 tablespoons chopped fresh
   rosemary
sea salt and freshly ground black
   pepper to taste
2 tablespoons olive oil
2 bunches asparagus, woody ends
   removed
8–10 skewers

TO SERVE

Yoghurt Sauce (see page 76)

Any excuse to crank the barbecue will see me cooking outside, and kebabs are always fun. I love the process of choosing what to have on them and stacking them up. It's such a simple idea, yet it looks like you have gone to such an effort. Making kebabs is also another smart way to use up any leftover vegetables from the week. If you're using wooden skewers, soak them in water before threading them with food so they won't burn during cooking.

For the salad, place all the ingredients in a bowl and toss to combine well. Set aside.

For the lamb kebabs, place all the ingredients, except the asparagus (and the skewers!), in a large bowl and toss to combine well. Thread a piece of lamb onto a skewer, followed by onion, zucchini and capsicum in layers until you have 3–4 pieces of lamb on each skewer.

Preheat a large frying pan over high heat or set the barbecue grill to high. Cook the kebabs for 4–5 minutes until browned on all sides (you may need to do them in batches). Set aside to rest for a few minutes while you grill the asparagus.

Place the asparagus in the pan or on the barbecue and cook for 2–3 minutes until lightly charred.

Serve the lamb kebabs with the herb salad and the grilled asparagus, and drizzle with yoghurt sauce.

SPINACH AND HALLOUMI SALAD

SERVES **4** • TIME TO MAKE **25 MINUTES**

2 tablespoons vegetable oil

4 cloves garlic, minced

2 zucchini, sliced lengthways

2 bunches asparagus, woody ends
  removed

200 g (7 oz) halloumi, thickly
  sliced

sea salt and freshly ground black
  pepper to taste

100 g (3½ oz) baby spinach leaves

1 avocado, peeled and chopped
  into chunks

1 punnet cherry tomatoes, halved

1 red onion, thinly sliced

1 spring onion, thinly sliced

2 tablespoons chopped pistachios

2 tablespoons balsamic glaze

**Now I don't like to play favourites, but when it comes
to salad I have to single out this one right here. The
combination of the warm pan-fried zucchini and asparagus
with the fresh cherry tomatoes, avocado and the crunch
of pistachios is just outstanding. Serve on its own or
alongside barbecued meat.**

Heat a large frying pan or barbecue grill plate over medium
heat. Place the oil, garlic, zucchini, asparagus and halloumi in a
large shallow dish, toss to coat the veges and halloumi in the
oil, and season. Place in the pan or on the grill and cook until
browned. Remove from the heat.

Arrange the spinach, avocado, tomatoes and onion on a large
serving platter. Mix through the grilled vegetables and halloumi,
scatter over the spring onion and pistachios, and drizzle with
balsamic glaze before serving.

PARMESAN-CRUMBED FISH WITH TOMATO RAGU

SERVES **4** • TIME TO MAKE **30 MINUTES**

ROAST POTATOES

1 kg (2 lb 4 oz) baby potatoes
2 tablespoons olive oil
sea salt to taste
2–3 sprigs rosemary

TOMATO RAGU

2 tablespoons olive oil
1 red onion, thickly sliced
3 cloves garlic, minced
1 red capsicum, deseeded and sliced
2 zucchini, sliced
½ cup pitted kalamata olives
1 cup tomato passata
400 g (14 oz) can chopped tomatoes
sea salt and freshly ground black
   pepper to taste

FISH

1 egg, lightly beaten
½ cup panko crumbs
¼ cup finely grated Parmesan
2 tablespoons finely chopped parsley
4 white fish fillets such as gurnard
   or terakihi (about 450 g / 1 lb)
1 tablespoon rice bran oil

TO SERVE

100 g (3½ oz) baby spinach leaves
1 lemon, cut into wedges

This recipe was inspired by a WOOP meal-kit dish I fell in love with and adapted over time. It is so easy to make, and the flavour combination is the bomb. White fish can sometimes lack excitement and flavour, but this dish really brings it to life.

Preheat the oven to 200°C (400°F) and place a roasting tray inside to heat.

For the roast potatoes, halve or quarter any large ones. Place the potato pieces in a large pot of cold salted water. Bring to the boil and cook for 10 minutes until beginning to soften. Drain well and place on the hot roasting tray. Drizzle with the olive oil and toss to coat. Season with salt, throw the rosemary on top and cook for 10–15 minutes until crispy.

For the tomato ragu, heat the olive oil in a large frying pan over medium-high heat. Add the onion, garlic, capsicum and zucchini and fry until golden. Add the olives, tomato passata and chopped tomatoes. Season, reduce the heat and cook for about 10 minutes until the vegetables are tender.

While the ragu and potatoes are cooking, prepare the fish. Place the egg in a bowl and combine the panko crumbs, Parmesan and half the parsley in another bowl. Coat each fish fillet with beaten egg, then dip it in the Parmesan crumbs. Heat the rice bran oil in a large non-stick frying pan over medium-high heat, add the fish and cook for 2–3 minutes each side.

Divide the spinach among serving plates. Top with potatoes and ragu and serve the fish on top, garnished with the remaining parsley and with lemon wedges for squeezing.

SHERRY AND ORANGE-GLAZED SALMON WITH CREAMY LEEK, KUMARA MASH AND KALE

SERVES **4** • TIME TO MAKE **30 MINUTES**

2 large kumara, peeled and
  chopped
1 tablespoon olive oil
2 tablespoons butter
2 leeks, sliced and rinsed
3 cloves garlic, minced
¼ teaspoon sea salt
¼ teaspoon freshly ground black
  pepper
½ cup cream
200 g (7 oz) kale, thick stalks
  removed and leaves torn

GLAZED SALMON

2 tablespoons sherry vinegar
½ cup fresh orange juice
1 tablespoon brown sugar
1 small orange, sliced
1 tablespoon vegetable oil
4 x 150 g (5½ oz) skin-on
  salmon fillets

The sound and smell of a fresh piece of salmon hitting a hot pan is one of the best things ever, and nothing beats that crispy skin and the flakiness of the delicate flesh when you take your first mouthful.

Place the kumara in a large pot of cold salted water. Bring to the boil, reduce the heat and cook for 10 minutes, or until very tender. Drain, return the kumara to the pot and cover.

While the kumara is cooking, heat the oil and half the butter in a large frying pan over medium-high heat. Add the leek, garlic and seasoning and cook for 5 minutes until the leeks begin to soften. Add the cream, reduce the heat and cook for another 5 minutes until thickened.

For the glaze, heat the vinegar, orange juice, sugar and orange slices in a small saucepan over a low heat for 5 minutes.

Heat the vegetable oil in a large heavy-based frying pan over medium-high heat. Add the salmon fillets, skin side down, and spoon over some of the glaze. Cook for 2–3 minutes, spoon over a little more glaze, then turn the fillets over. Spoon over more glaze and cook for another 2–3 minutes. Remove the salmon from the pan and set aside to rest for a few minutes. Add the kale to the pan with 1–2 tablespoons of the glaze and cook for 3–4 minutes until wilted.

Mash the kumara with the remaining tablespoon of butter, season and divide among serving plates. Top with the creamed leek and salmon fillets. Spoon over the remaining glaze, including the orange slices, and serve immediately.

CAULIFLOWER AND YOGHURT PIZZAS

SERVES **4** • TIME TO MAKE **1 HOUR**

1 large head cauliflower, cut into
small florets
2 cups plain unsweetened yoghurt
4 cups self-raising flour, plus extra
for dusting
¼ teaspoon sea salt
2 cloves garlic, minced (optional)
¼ cup pizza sauce
1 red onion, sliced
1 cup sliced mushrooms
1 cup sliced capsicum
1 cup quartered cherry tomatoes
½ cup grated mozzarella per pizza
2 teaspoons dried mixed herbs or
fresh oregano and parsley
fresh herbs to garnish (e.g. basil,
parsley or oregano)

These pizza bases taste great and have a really nice texture to them—you can barely tell cauliflower has been used. Pack them with all your favourite pizza toppings and you are set for a fab night in. It's also a good opportunity to use up bits and pieces from your fridge.

You can also use the dough to make flatbread or garlic or herb bread—once it's pressed out just bake for 12–15 minutes, or until golden brown.

Preheat the oven to 240°C (475°F). Line 2 oven trays with baking paper and dust with flour.

Cook the cauliflower in a pot of boiling water until tender. Drain well, then put into a food processor with the yoghurt. Blitz until smooth. Add the flour, salt and garlic to the food processor and mix until a dough forms. It will be quite sticky but that's fine.

Transfer the dough to a floured surface and divide into quarters. You can either make 4 pizzas or make 2 pizzas and freeze the other 2 balls.

For the pizza bases, transfer 1 dough ball to each oven tray and, with well-floured hands, press the dough out to approx. 30 cm (12 in) diameter each. Cook for 5 minutes.

Remove the bases from the oven and carefully spread over the pizza sauce. Arrange the onion, mushroom, capsicum and tomatoes over the top. Sprinkle over the mozzarella and dried herbs.

Cook for another 10 minutes until the cheese is golden and bubbling. Serve immediately topped with fresh herbs.

BEEF STROGANOFF WITH PAPPARDELLE

SERVES **4–6** • TIME TO MAKE **APPROX. 3 HOURS**

2 tablespoons olive oil
250 g (9 oz) rindless shoulder
  bacon, cut into 5 cm (2 in) strips
500 g (1 lb 2 oz) beef strips
sea salt and freshly ground black
  pepper to taste
2 onions, cut into wedges
250 g (9 oz) brown button
  mushrooms, halved
5 cloves garlic, roughly chopped
1 teaspoon smoked paprika
400 g (14 oz) can tomato soup
  concentrate
400 g (14 oz) can chopped
  tomatoes
1 tablespoon Worcestershire
  sauce
¼ cup sour cream
250 g (9 oz) pappardelle
2 tablespoons finely chopped
  parsley and/or chives

This recipe comes from my talented mumma, Nikki. It takes me straight back to our family home, where we ate the most incredible home-cooked meals every night. Mum and Dad put every inch of their souls into making that house feel like home. This stroganoff was a staple—it's hearty, warming and makes the best comfort meal in winter.

Heat half the oil in a large frying pan over high heat. Add the bacon and cook until browned. Transfer the bacon to a 3-litre slow cooker and reserve the pan. If using an oven, transfer the bacon to a large ovenproof dish and set aside, then preheat the oven to 160°C (315°F).

Season the beef strips. In 2 batches, add the beef to the pan and brown over high heat. Transfer to the slow cooker or oven dish.

Heat the remaining tablespoon of oil in the same pan over medium-high heat. Add the onion and mushrooms and cook, stirring, for 5 minutes. Add the garlic and paprika and cook for another minute. Transfer to the slow cooker or oven dish.

Pour the tomato soup, tomatoes and Worcestershire sauce over the beef mixture and stir to combine. Cover and cook on medium in the slow cooker or in the oven for 2–3 hours, or until the beef is very tender.

When it's nearly time to serve the stroganoff, cook the pappardelle according to the packet instructions.

Stir the sour cream into the stroganoff and season to taste. Serve with the pappardelle, and sprinkle with parsley or chives.

PARMESAN, RICOTTA AND EGGPLANT INVOLTINI

SERVES **4** • TIME TO MAKE **40 MINUTES**

TOMATO SAUCE

2 tablespoons olive oil
1 onion, diced
2 cloves garlic, minced
1 teaspoon dried oregano
400 g (14 oz) can chopped
   tomatoes
150 g (5½ oz) spinach, chopped
1 tablespoon brown sugar
1 tablespoon Worcestershire
   sauce
sea salt and freshly ground black
   pepper to taste

INVOLTINI

3 large eggplants
olive oil spray
sea salt
400 g (14 oz) ricotta
2 eggs, whisked
½ cup finely grated Parmesan
1 teaspoon ground nutmeg
2 tablespoons fresh thyme leaves,
   plus extra to serve
¼ teaspoon salt
¼ teaspoon cracked pepper
1 cup grated mozzarella

Eggplant involtini is the perfect Italian comfort food. Think lasagne, but with eggplant in place of the pasta, and with the other layers wrapped up inside. Involtini translates to 'small parcels or rolls' in English and that explains how you make these little packages of goodness.

Preheat the oven to 200°C (400°F) and line 2 large oven trays with baking paper.

For the tomato sauce, heat the oil in a large saucepan over medium heat. Add the onion, garlic and oregano and cook until fragrant. Add the tomatoes, spinach, sugar, Worcestershire sauce and seasoning. Reduce the heat and simmer for about 15 minutes. Remove from the heat.

For the involtini, remove the stem ends of the eggplants and slice lengthways into ½ cm (¼ in) slices—you should have about 20 large slices to roll. Place on the prepared oven trays, spray with olive oil and season with salt. Bake for 10–15 minutes until soft.

Mix the ricotta, egg, Parmesan, nutmeg, thyme, salt and pepper together in a bowl. Place a dessertspoonful of mix on each eggplant slice and roll up to make involtini.

Spoon the tomato sauce into a 5–10 cm (2–4 in) deep ovenproof dish. Press the involtini lightly into the sauce and sprinkle over the mozzarella. Bake for 15–20 minutes, or until golden and bubbling.

Sprinkle over the extra thyme leaves and serve with a leafy green salad.

CHICKEN AND LEEK POT PIE

SERVES **4 (OR MAKES 4 INDIVIDUAL PIES)** • TIME TO MAKE **1 HOUR**

1 tablespoon olive oil

400 g (14 oz) chicken thigh fillets, skinned, boned and chopped into 2 cm (¾ in) cubes

2 tablespoons butter

2 leeks, sliced

2 cloves garlic, minced

1 heaped teaspoon dried thyme

¼ cup plain flour, plus extra for dusting

2 cups sliced button mushrooms

1½ cups warmed milk

sea salt and freshly ground black pepper to taste

olive oil spray

2 sheets flaky pastry

1 egg, lightly beaten

2 teaspoons sesame seeds

TO SERVE

salad leaves

relish of your choice

The ultimate meal for a cold winter's day: digging into one of these crispy pies will make you feel instantly warmer inside. I grew up making pies in my grandmother's kitchen, helping her roll out the pastry and cutting out (uneven) initials to go on top. To me this pie means happiness and family—it makes me feel safe and my heart content.

Preheat the oven to 180°C (350°F). Heat the oil in a large non-stick frying pan over medium heat. In batches, add the chicken and cook for 4–5 minutes, or until golden. Remove the chicken from the pan, set aside and keep warm.

Add the butter, leeks, garlic and thyme to the pan and cook over medium heat for about 10 minutes, or until the leeks have softened. Add the flour and cook for 2 minutes, stirring every 30 seconds. Add the mushrooms, milk, salt and pepper and cook, stirring regularly, for a further 3 minutes, or until the sauce has thickened. Return the chicken to the sauce and mix gently to combine. Refrigerate until cooled to room temperature.

Lightly spray a 20 cm (8 in) pie dish with oil and pour in the cooled chicken mixture, or divide it among 4 individual pie tins.

On a floured surface, join the 2 pastry sheets and roll out slightly to make a bigger sheet. Place the pastry on top of the pie dish and trim the excess around the sides of the dish. If you're making individual pies cut 2 circles to fit your pie dishes out of each sheet of pastry.

Prick the pastry lid with a fork, then brush with the egg. Sprinkle with sesame seeds and bake for 30–40 minutes, or until the pastry is golden. Serve with salad and relish.

SLOW-COOKED LAMB SHANKS

SERVES **4** • TIME TO MAKE **6–8 HOURS (SLOW COOKER) OR 3 HOURS (OVEN)**

4 lamb shanks
½ teaspoon salt
½ teaspoon cracked black pepper
2 teaspoons dried chilli flakes
1 teaspoon ground coriander
1 teaspoon dried oregano
1 tablespoon flour
1 tablespoon olive oil
3 cloves garlic, minced
2 large carrots, peeled and sliced
4 stalks celery, sliced
2 large onions, cut into wedges
1 tablespoon chopped fresh
  rosemary
2 tablespoons balsamic vinegar
1 cup dry white wine
2 x 400 g (14 oz) cans chopped
  tomatoes
2 cups chicken stock
1 kg (2 lb 4 oz) mashing potatoes,
  peeled and quartered
dash of milk (optional)
small bunch fresh basil or Italian
  parsley, roughly chopped

Another one that comes straight from the kitchen of my beautiful mum, Nikki. The meat falls off the bone and is so tender and juicy. If you're organising your next date night with a special partner, this is the one to dazzle them with.

Preheat the oven to 180°C (350°F).

Season the lamb shanks. Mix the chilli, coriander and oregano into the flour. Roll the lamb in this mixture, pressing it in well.

Heat the oil in a large cast-iron casserole dish over medium heat, add the lamb and brown on all sides. Remove from the pan and set aside.

Add the garlic, carrot, celery, onion, rosemary and a pinch of salt to the casserole dish and cook until the vegetables have softened. Add the balsamic vinegar and allow it to reduce for about 1 minute. Pour in the white wine and simmer for 2 minutes. Add the tomatoes and stock, stir to combine, then add the lamb shanks.

Transfer the shanks and sauce to a slow cooker and cook on low for at least 6–8 hours. If not using a slow cooker, bring to a boil, cover, and place in the oven for about 2 hours, or until the lamb is falling off the bone. Remove the lid and cook for a further 20 minutes.

About 20 minutes before serving, place the potato chunks into a large pot of cold salted water. Bring to the boil and cook until tender. Mash until smooth. Add some milk for a creamier texture, if desired.

Skim any excess fat off the lamb shanks and season. Stir in the basil or parsley, and serve with the mashed potato.

PESTO CHICKEN WITH POTATOES AND ROCKET SALAD

SERVES **2** • TIME TO MAKE **40 MINUTES**

4 boneless, skinless chicken thighs
  (approx. 400 g / 14 oz)
½ cup pesto
½ cup grated mozzarella
500 g (1 lb 2 oz) baby potatoes,
  halved or quartered if large
2 tablespoons olive oil
sea salt and freshly ground black
  pepper to taste
2 tablespoons rosemary leaves
2 cups rocket leaves
1 small red onion, thinly sliced
1 cup cherry tomatoes, halved
½ cucumber, thinly sliced
50 g (1¾ oz) feta, crumbled

Pesto has to be one of the best things for adding flavour to a dish. This recipe uses storebought pesto to speed things up on those nights when you need dinner in a hurry. That said, I do encourage you to try making your own pesto when you have the time—the flavour you get is next level.

Preheat the oven to 180°C (350°F) and line an oven tray with baking paper.

Place the chicken thighs on a board, dollop 1 teaspoon pesto onto each and sprinkle over some mozzarella. Roll each thigh up snugly, secure with a skewer and place on the prepared tray along with the potatoes. Drizzle everything with the olive oil, and scatter the rosemary leaves over the potatoes. Season and cook for 20 minutes, or until the chicken is golden and cooked through.

Place the rocket, red onion, tomatoes, cucumber and feta in a bowl and toss with the remaining pesto to combine.

Serve the chicken and potatoes on top of the salad.

FETTUCCINE WITH BOLOGNAISE SAUCE

SERVES **4** • TIME TO MAKE **1 HOUR**

2 tablespoons olive oil
1 onion, diced
2 cloves garlic, minced
2 stalks celery, finely diced
1 carrot, peeled and finely
  chopped
500 g (1 lb 2 oz) beef mince
½ cup red wine
1 tablespoon Worcestershire
  sauce
1 cup salt-reduced beef stock
400 g (14 oz) can tomato purée
400 g (14 oz) can chopped
  tomatoes
1 teaspoon dried oregano
sea salt and freshly grated black
  pepper to taste
400 g (14 oz) dried fettuccine
½ cup Parmesan shavings
½ cup chopped parsley leaves

You can never go wrong with this fancy spag bol! It was one of the very first meals I learnt to make as a kid— thinking I was a big help to Mum when in reality I was just slowing her down and getting in the way. I loved feeding the fettuccine into the big pot of water and watching the strands turn soft and silky. And of course I had to taste-test the Parmesan multiple times just to check it was okay. Actually, I still do this . . .

Heat the oil in a large frying pan over medium-high heat. Add the onion, garlic, celery and carrot, and cook for 5 minutes until the veges are soft and starting to colour.

Add the mince to the pan and fry until browned, about 5 minutes.

Add the red wine (it will spit a little so wear an apron) and cook out for 1 minute. Stir in the Worcestershire sauce, stock, tomato purée, chopped tomatoes and dried oregano. Reduce the heat and simmer gently for 20–30 minutes until thickened. Remove from the heat, season then cover with a lid and set aside for 10 minutes.

While the sauce is resting, bring a large pot of salted water to the boil, add the pasta and cook for 10–12 minutes until al dente. Drain the pasta, then return to the pan with the sauce and toss to combine. Alternatively, divide the pasta among bowls and top with the sauce. Garnish with Parmesan and parsley before serving.

BUNLESS
BURGERS

500 g (1 lb 2 oz) beef mince
1 onion, finely chopped
1 carrot, grated
1 zucchini, grated
½ cup chopped parsley leaves
2 eggs, whisked
2 tablespoons grainy mustard
2 teaspoons paprika
½ teaspoon sea salt
freshly ground black pepper to
  taste
olive oil spray
8 large iceberg lettuce leaves
½ cucumber, peeled into ribbons
1 red capsicum, deseeded and
  sliced
2 tomatoes, sliced
1 avocado, peeled and sliced
1 red onion, thinly sliced
beetroot relish

It's not until you try a bunless burger that you realise you've been wasting your time on consuming the bun. You honestly won't even notice the difference—these are just as tasty and you'll be able to fit in even more vegetables.

Place the mince, onion, carrot, zucchini, parsley, egg, mustard and paprika in a large bowl and season. Mix together until well combined. Form the mixture into 4 patties, place on a large plate and refrigerate for at least 20 minutes.

Preheat the oven to 180°C (350°F) and line an oven tray with baking paper.

Spray the patties with a little oil and place on the prepared oven tray. Bake for 15–20 minutes, or until cooked through.

Serve the burger patties inside the lettuce leaves topped with cucumber, capsicum, tomato, avocado, onion and some beetroot relish.

CHICKEN AND PRAWN LAKSA

SERVES **4** • TIME TO MAKE **40 MINUTES**

350 g (12 oz) rice noodles

2 tablespoons sesame oil

1 tablespoon finely grated fresh ginger

2 cloves garlic, minced

zest and juice of 1 lime, plus extra lime wedges to serve

2 tablespoons laksa paste

2 cups salt-reduced chicken stock

400 ml (14 fl oz) can light coconut milk

1 tablespoon brown sugar

1 tablespoon fish sauce

1 red chilli

2 tomatoes, diced

400 g (14 oz) boneless, skinless chicken thighs, very thinly sliced

12 prawns, heads removed

2 cups baby spinach

¼ teaspoon sea salt

¼ teaspoon freshly ground black pepper

2 Lebanese cucumbers, peeled into ribbons

150 g (5½ oz) mung bean sprouts

2 spring onions, thinly sliced

½ cup coriander

½ cup mint leaves

1 red chilli, thinly sliced

4 hard-boiled eggs, halved

If you look through my cooking highlights on social media, laksa features heavily. I've tried a variety of recipes and methods and have landed on this, my all-time favourite. In the past I have made the laksa paste from scratch, but unless you have a wild herb garden that process can be timely and expensive. These days I use a laksa paste from the supermarket.

Cook the noodles according to the packet instructions. Drain, rinse and set aside to soak in cold water.

Heat the oil in a large pot over medium heat and add the ginger, garlic, lime zest and laksa paste. Cook, stirring, for 1 minute, then add the stock, coconut milk, sugar, fish sauce, chilli and tomato. Simmer for 5 minutes, add the chicken, reduce the heat to low and cook for another 5 minutes until the chicken is cooked through. Stir the prawns and spinach into the laksa, add the lime juice and season.

Toss the cucumber, bean sprouts, spring onion, coriander, mint and chilli together on a platter and place the hard-boiled eggs on a plate. Drain the rice noodles and divide them among serving bowls. Pour over the laksa, and serve with veges and eggs on the side for your guests to help themselves.

GRILLED MASALA FISH WITH PINEAPPLE SALSA

SERVES **4** • TIME TO MAKE **30 MINUTES**

COCONUT RICE

1½ cups basmati rice
1 cup coconut milk
2 cups water
pinch of salt
2 tablespoons coconut chips

FISH AND GREENS

1 tablespoon vegetable oil
1 tablespoon ground garam masala
4 large white fish fillets (approx.
  600 g / 1 lb 5 oz)
4 small bok choy or pak choy,
  halved lengthways
2 bunches asparagus, woody ends
  removed
1 teaspoon sesame oil
1 tablespoon soy sauce

TO SERVE

Pineapple Salsa (see page 154)
1 tablespoon toasted sesame
  seeds
¼ cup roughly chopped toasted
  cashews
coriander leaves
1 lime, cut into wedges

Sitting on the deck in the golden hour of a summer's evening with a glass of rosé in hand, Trent by my side and little Maddox at my feet, hoping for spillage—that's how I love to enjoy this dish best. Cooking the fish on the barbecue also means you can keep any fishy smells outside.

For the coconut rice, place the rice in a sieve and rinse well. Place in a large pot or a rice cooker with the coconut milk, water and salt. Stir, place the lid on the pot and bring to the boil. Reduce the heat and simmer for about 12–15 minutes until all the liquid has been absorbed and the rice is tender but not mushy. Add a little water to the pot if it looks like it needs it towards the end of cooking. Stir the coconut chips through the rice, keep covered and set aside.

For the fish and greens, preheat the barbecue grill plate or frying pan to medium and bring a large pot of water to the boil. Rub the oil and garam masala over the fish fillets. Cook the fish on the barbecue or in the frying pan for 1–2 minutes on each side, depending on the size of the fillets.

While the fish is cooking, add the bok choy and asparagus to the boiling water and cook for 1 minute until wilting but still a little crunchy. Drain well, put in a bowl with the sesame oil and soy sauce and toss to coat. Put the vegetables onto the hot grill or pan and sear lightly.

Divide the coconut rice, fish, greens and salsa among serving plates. Garnish with sesame seeds, cashews and coriander, and serve with lime wedges for squeezing.

SATAY CHICKEN RICE PAPER WRAPS

SERVES **4** • TIME TO MAKE **25 MINUTES**

SATAY SAUCE

½ cup pineapple juice

400 ml (14 fl oz) can coconut milk

1 cup smooth peanut butter

½ cup sweet chilli sauce

2 tablespoons soy sauce

zest and juice of 1 lime

1 tablespoon finely grated fresh
  ginger

1 stalk lemongrass, cut in half
  lengthways, or 1 teaspoon minced
  lemongrass from a jar

WRAPS

500 g (1 lb 2 oz) chicken thighs,
  thinly sliced

1 teaspoon peanut oil

1 pack large rice paper wraps

1 head cos lettuce, leaves torn

2 cups mung bean sprouts

1 avocado, peeled and sliced

1 red capsicum, deseeded and thinly
  sliced

2 carrots, peeled and cut into long
  matchsticks

1 cucumber, cut into long
  matchsticks

1 cup mint leaves, plus extra to serve

1 cup coriander leaves

1 lime, cut into wedges, to serve

If you're a friend of mine and you've been invited over for dinner, I can guarantee that you have eaten these little morsels at some stage. This recipe is hands down my all-time favourite. Trust me, these wraps taste incredible.

I often serve these when I entertain as it's easy to get everyone involved. I set up a big platter of all the ingredients and let my guests assemble their own wraps, filling them with whatever they like.

For the satay sauce, place the ingredients in a saucepan and heat gently. Whisk until combined and remove from the heat.

Mix the chicken and ¼ cup of the satay sauce in a bowl, coating the chicken well. Heat the peanut oil in a frying pan over medium heat. Add the chicken and cook for 3–4 minutes until the chicken is cooked through.

Fill a large bowl with warm water and set out a clean, damp tea towel. Dip the rice paper wrappers into the water one at a time for 2–3 seconds to soften and lay out on the tea towel. Layer some of the chicken, lettuce, sprouts, avocado, capsicum, carrot, cucumber and herbs along the centre of each wrap. Fold in the two (shorter) opposite sides of the wrapper to meet the filling. Then fold the bottom of the wrapper over the top of the filling and roll up.

Serve the wraps with the remaining satay sauce for dipping and lime wedges for squeezing.

BROCCOLI AND BACON SALAD WITH GOAT'S CHEESE AND POMEGRANATE

SERVES **4** • TIME TO MAKE **15 MINUTES**

MUSTARD DRESSING

½ cup Greek yoghurt
2 teaspoons wholegrain mustard
zest and juice of 1 lemon
sea salt and freshly ground black
  pepper to taste

SALAD

1 head broccoli, cut into small
  florets
4 rashers shoulder bacon, rind
  removed
2 cups rocket
1 red onion, thinly sliced
1 punnet cherry tomatoes, halved
½ cup chopped almonds
½ cup pomegranate arils
120 g (4¼ oz) creamy goat's
  cheese
½ cup chopped Italian parsley

Tonight you are bringing home the bacon . . . literally. If you have a member of your family who refuses salads, this little number will be their gateway salad. With the full flavour from the bacon and the crunch and sweetness from the pomegranate, you've got a combination that will get everyone excited about having salad for dinner.

For the dressing, mix all the ingredients together in a bowl. Set aside.

For the salad, bring a large pot of salted water to the boil. Carefully drop in the broccoli and cook for 2 minutes until just tender. Drain and place the broccoli in a serving dish.

Heat a non-stick frying pan over medium-high heat. Add the bacon and cook for about 2 minutes each side until crispy. When cool enough to handle, chop the bacon into small pieces and set aside.

Add the rocket, onion, tomatoes, almonds, pomegranate and dressing to the dish with the broccoli, and toss to combine. Sprinkle over the chopped bacon and crumble over the goat's cheese. Garnish with the parsley before serving.

Snacks and treats

CARROT FRIES

3 large carrots, ends removed and
  peeled
¼ cup finely grated Parmesan
1 tablespoon garlic powder
2 tablespoons olive oil
2 tablespoons chopped parsley
  leaves
sea salt and freshly ground black
  pepper to taste
Yoghurt Sauce (see page 76)

**These carrot fries are loaded with all the tastiness of
French fries while still having all the health benefits
of carrots. They make a great snack on their own or a
delicious accompaniment to any meal. When we entertain
friends I often make these to serve as a starter before
dinner.**

Preheat the oven to 200°C (400°F) and line an oven tray with
baking paper.

Cut the carrots into long fry-shaped sticks (you should get
about 8 per carrot). Place the sticks in a large shallow bowl with
the Parmesan, garlic powder, olive oil, parsley and seasoning.
Toss well to coat the carrot sticks completely. Transfer the
carrots to the prepared oven tray and drizzle over any extra
Parmesan mixture.

Bake the carrots for 20 minutes until they are soft and the
coating is a golden brown.

Serve the carrot fries hot with the yoghurt sauce.

LOW-CARB HUMMUS AND CHICKEN CUCUMBER ROLLS

MAKES **12 ROLLS** • TIME TO MAKE **10 MINUTES**

1 cucumber, ends removed, peeled and halved

½ cup Hummus (see page 84)

1 cooked chicken breast, shredded

1 capsicum, deseeded and thinly sliced

½ cup baby spinach, roughly chopped

2 small tomatoes, sliced into wedges

sea salt and freshly ground black pepper to taste

dill and parsley leaves, to garnish (optional)

toothpicks

Could these be any cuter? Just look how impressive these little dudes are. They remind me of something you would see when you're treated to a five-star dining experience, but they are so simple to create at home with just a few ingredients and some toothpicks.

Peel the cucumber halves into strips and lay out on a large board.

Spread each strip with hummus, then divide the chicken, capsicum, spinach and tomato among the strips. Season with salt and pepper and carefully roll up each strip.

Secure with toothpicks, garnish with dill and parsley, if desired, and serve immediately.

KALE CHIPS

SERVES **4** • TIME TO MAKE **15 MINUTES**

100 g (3½ oz) large kale leaves, washed, dried well and stems removed
1 tablespoon lemon juice
1 tablespoon olive oil
½ teaspoon smoked paprika
½ teaspoon caster sugar
½ teaspoon salt

Don't judge a book by its cover, and definitely don't judge these bad boys until you've given them a try. One of my very first posts on my Journey to Health Facebook page was about making these for the first time. I was surprised at how easy they were to make and just how delicious they are. A kale chip gives you the same satisfaction and crunch of a standard potato chip, while being a whole lot better for you. Make them fresh and eat them straight away, as they don't keep well.

Preheat the oven to 180°C (350°F) and line a large oven tray with baking paper.

Tear the kale leaves into pieces and place in a large bowl. Drizzle over the lemon juice and use your hands to massage it into the kale pieces to tenderise them. Add the remaining ingredients and mix with your hands to coat.

Spread the kale out on the prepared oven tray, sprinkle with a little more salt and bake for 10 minutes, or until you notice the edges of the leaves start to brown.

Remove from the oven and transfer the chips to a cooling rack to crisp up for 5 minutes, then serve immediately.

BAKED TORTILLA CHIPS

MAKES **ABOUT 16–20 CHIPS FROM EACH WRAP** • TIME TO MAKE **10 MINUTES**

1 packet large wraps or tortillas

Whenever I open a packet of wraps there are always one or two left over that I never seem to get through. Not wanting to waste them (and knowing that they don't freeze well), I've found this fun way to use them up.

You can spray the shapes with a little olive oil spray and sprinkle over a dash of salt before baking, but if you want to be super healthy just bake them as they are. Dip the chips into your favourite hummus or pesto and you have the easiest snack. You can also use them as the base for nachos.

Preheat the oven to 180°C (350°F) and line 2 large oven trays with baking paper.

Using cookie cutters or a sharp knife, cut shapes into the wraps and place on the prepared oven trays. Cook for 5–8 minutes, watching carefully so they don't burn.

Leave to cool on cooling racks and store in an airtight container. They will keep for at least 2 weeks.

PISTACHIO PESTO

MAKES **1 CUP** • TIME TO MAKE **5 MINUTES**

½ cup mint leaves
½ cup basil leaves
½ cup light olive oil
zest and juice of 1 lemon
½ cup chopped pistachios, plus
  extra to serve
3 cloves garlic

This pesto is packed full of flavour. I like to keep blitzing until the mixture is almost smooth with just a few little chunks in it, but you can stop the food processor sooner to get the texture you prefer. This is a perfect match with my Baked Tortilla Chips (see page 150).

Place all the ingredients in a food processor. Blitz until you reach your desired texture. The pesto will keep in an airtight container in the fridge for up to 2 weeks.

SATAY CHICKEN NIBBLES WITH PINEAPPLE SALSA

MAKES **APPROX. 16 NIBBLES** • TIME TO MAKE **30 MINUTES**

PINEAPPLE SALSA

2 cups finely diced fresh pineapple
1 red chilli, finely chopped
1 cup fresh or defrosted frozen
    corn kernels
¼ cup chopped mint
¼ cup coriander leaves
1 spring onion, thinly sliced
juice of 1 lime
sea salt and freshly ground black
    pepper to taste

CHICKEN NIBBLES

1 kg (2 lb 4 oz) chicken nibbles
1 tablespoon olive oil
pinch of salt
Satay Sauce (see page 138)

TO GARNISH

handful coriander leaves
chopped red chilli

When Trent and I were travelling around Bali our dishes were often served with a delicious salsa, and I would always ask the cafés and restaurants what they used in theirs and keep a note. When I got home I started playing in the kitchen and I came up with this pineapple salsa. It tastes extra incredible when paired with your good mate the chicken nibbles.

Preheat the oven to 200°C (400°F) and line a large oven tray with baking paper.

For the salsa, combine all the ingredients in a bowl, cover and refrigerate until ready to serve.

For the chicken, place the nibbles in a large bowl, drizzle over the oil and salt and stir to coat. Place in a single layer on the prepared oven tray and bake for 20 minutes until the nibbles are cooked through with crispy skin. Remove the nibbles from the oven and keep the oven on.

Dip the cooked chicken nibbles in the satay sauce to coat and lay back on the oven tray. Place back in the oven for another 5 minutes until the sauce is lightly browned.

Serve the chicken nibbles with the pineapple salsa and remaining satay sauce. Garnish with the coriander and chilli before serving.

BROCCOLI BALLS

SERVES **2** • TIME TO MAKE **30 MINUTES**

1 head broccoli, cut into small
   florets and stalk thinly sliced
1 egg
⅓ cup grated Cheddar
⅔ cup panko crumbs
½ brown onion, finely diced
2 tablespoons chopped parsley
   leaves
sea salt and freshly ground black
   pepper to taste

TO SERVE

½ cup tomato relish
Yoghurt Sauce (see page 76)

I swear anything made into a ball just tastes better, doesn't it? There is something about a bite-sized mouthful that is super appealing, and these are so yummy that even the anti-broccoli community will want to give them a go. Be warned: kids go wild for these, so get ready to be pestered to make them again and again.

Preheat the oven to 200°C (400°F) and line an oven tray with baking paper. Bring a full kettle of water to the boil.

Place the broccoli in a large bowl and pour over the boiling water to cover. Leave for 1 minute then drain well. Place the broccoli in a food processor and blitz until very finely chopped but not puréed.

Place the chopped broccoli in a large bowl with all the other ingredients and mix until combined. Roll the broccoli mixture into small balls and place on the prepared oven tray.

Bake the broccoli balls for 10 minutes. Flip the balls over and cook for a further 10 minutes until golden brown.

Serve the broccoli balls hot with your favourite tomato relish and the yoghurt sauce.

FROZEN GRAPES

SERVES **6** • TIME TO MAKE **2 MINUTES, PLUS 2–3 HOURS FREEZING TIME**

1 bunch red or green grapes, or a mix

Now I realise that this is not exactly a recipe—or even something that needs explaining—but I swear this little trick changed my life. I shared this hack on my Instagram stories and it *blew up*. I have never been tagged in more stories on a single topic!

We all have those times when we feel like something sweet, and these frozen grapes make the perfect alternative to lollies or chocolate. They genuinely taste like little frozen sweets. You can try this with most other fruit, too.

Once frozen, store the grapes in a sealable bag or lidded container for a snack on the go.

Line a large oven tray with baking paper.

Spread the grapes out into a single layer on the prepared tray. Pop in the freezer and wait until frozen before eating.

PEANUT BUTTER AND CACAO NIB PROTEIN BLISS BALLS

MAKES **20** • TIME TO MAKE **10 MINUTES, PLUS REFRIGERATION TIME**

1 cup desiccated coconut
1 tablespoon vanilla protein power
2 tablespoons peanut butter
1 cup almond meal
½ cup oats
½ cup cacao nibs
½ cup Medjool dates, softened in
  ¼ cup boiling water
1 tablespoon good-quality maple
  syrup
1 teaspoon vanilla extract
¼ teaspoon sea salt

If you open my freezer you'll always find a large container filled with these delicious little beauties. They are the best snack to have on hand: they freeze beautifully (will keep for up to 2 months) and are packed full of protein to keep your energy levels up. The ideal companion to your evening cup of tea.

Place the desiccated coconut on a plate and set aside.

Place all the remaining ingredients in a high-powered blender or food processor and blend to combine.

Roll tablespoonfuls of the mixture into balls, roll in the coconut to coat and refrigerate until firm.

HEALTHY ZUCCHINI AND BANANA MUFFINS

MAKES **12** • TIME TO MAKE **25 MINUTES**

1 large zucchini, grated
1 large banana, peeled and
  mashed
¼ cup honey
¼ cup melted coconut oil
1 teaspoon vanilla extract
2 large eggs
⅓ cup dark chocolate chips
1 teaspoon ground cinnamon
½ teaspoon baking soda
½ teaspoon baking powder
¼ teaspoon salt
2 cups wholewheat flour

Zucchini in a muffin . . . who would have thought? These beauties are such a great way to get veges into fussy children or maybe even a fussy partner. Whip up a batch on the weekend and freeze them for easy midweek snack options. You can swap out the chocolate chips for berries or nuts if you'd prefer. I love to eat them sliced and spread with butter.

Preheat the oven to 180°C (350°F) and line a 12-hole muffin tin with muffin cases.

Place the zucchini on a clean dry tea towel, gather up the sides and squeeze out as much excess moisture as you can.

Place the banana, honey, coconut oil, vanilla and eggs in a large bowl and beat until smooth. Add the zucchini and chocolate chips and stir until combined.

Sift all the dry ingredients into the wet mix and fold everything together until all the flour has disappeared.

Divide the mix among the muffin cases, filling them two-thirds of the way. Bake for 15 minutes until a skewer inserted in the middle comes out clean. Cool the muffins on a cooling rack before eating or storing, or eat still warm if preferred.

PEANUT BUTTER AND CACAO NIB PROTEIN COOKIES

MAKES **16** • TIME TO MAKE **25 MINUTES**

⅓ cup peanut butter

¼ cup good-quality maple syrup

½ teaspoon pure vanilla extract

2 tablespoons vanilla or chocolate protein powder

¼ cup coconut sugar

¼ cup cacao nibs

¼ teaspoon salt

¼ teaspoon baking soda

½ cup coconut flour

1 egg plus 1 egg white, lightly beaten

It's 3 p.m., your energy levels are sinking and all you feel like is a sweet treat. These cookies are your best friend for times like this. Sweet enough to satisfy any cravings but with no refined sugar, they are packed full of protein and will easily see you through to dinner time.

Preheat the oven to 180°C (350°F) and line a large oven tray with baking paper.

Place the peanut butter, maple syrup and vanilla extract in a small saucepan and heat, stirring, until just combined.

Place all the dry ingredients in a large bowl, stir to combine and pour over the peanut butter mixture. Add the eggs and stir until a dough forms.

Roll tablespoonfuls of the mix into balls, flatten lightly between your palms and place on the prepared oven tray. Bake for 10–12 minutes. Allow to cool slightly and firm up before eating.

ACKNOWLEDGEMENTS

This project would not have been possible without a large team of amazing humans who made my dream a reality. Firstly, thank you to the Allen & Unwin team for having faith in me, not once but twice. Your help and guidance along the way has been invaluable and I appreciate each and every staff member—you truly are a well-oiled machine.

Thanks also to Jo, the talented food stylist who perfected every single food shot to ensure it looked cookbook worthy, as well as selecting and sourcing a stunning range of props from Delivision Food Styling, Hayley Bridgford Ceramics, Città and French Country. You even went the extra mile by allowing your beautiful daughter Emily to be the child model for our 'kids platter' photo. Jo, your wit and humour made every day of shooting a joy, and I loved every second of working alongside you. I could not have done this without you.

This leads me to Mel, who shot every single image in this book, including the cover and author photos. Mel, your attention to detail astounds me. Your passion shines through in your work, and I think this was evident when my instant reaction to every image you took was, *This has to be my new favourite!* I loved working with you . . . and your funky boots.

To my mother and grandmother, thank you for your patience and your love, and for passing on your love of food and cooking. I hope to one day have the same influence on the special people in my life.

Finally, to Trent: no words can ever capture the love and kindness you give to me and the support you show me in everything I do. Never once have you tried to dull my shine; instead you choose to ignite it, making me shine brighter by letting me know you have my back all the way. By the time this book is published and you are reading these words you will be my husband (that feels crazy to type!). I love you, baby—here's to a lifetime of adventure and good times.

INDEX

Note: Simone uses New Zealand standard measures, including the 15 ml (3 teaspoon) tablespoon. If you are using a larger Australian 20 ml (4 teaspoon) tablespoon, remove a teaspoon of ingredient for each tablespoon specified.

First published in 2020

Text © Simone Anderson Pretscherer, 2020
Photography © Melanie Jenkins (Flash Studios), 2020

Allen & Unwin
Level 2, 10 College Hill, Freemans Bay
Auckland 1011, New Zealand
Phone: (64 9) 377 3800
Email: auckland@allenandunwin.com
Web: www.allenandunwin.co.nz

83 Alexander Street
Crows Nest NSW 2065, Australia
Phone: (61 2) 8425 0100

A catalogue record for this book is available from the National Library of New Zealand.

ISBN 978 1 98854 743 5
UK ISBN 978 1 92235 114 2

Recipe development and styling by Jo Bridgford
(Delivision Food Styling)
Design by Kate Barraclough
Set in Europa
Printed in China by C & C Offset Printing Co. Ltd

10 9 8 7 6 5 4 3 2 1